CW01455223

Bakewell

Chatsworth and Haddon

Karl Barton & Louise Maskill

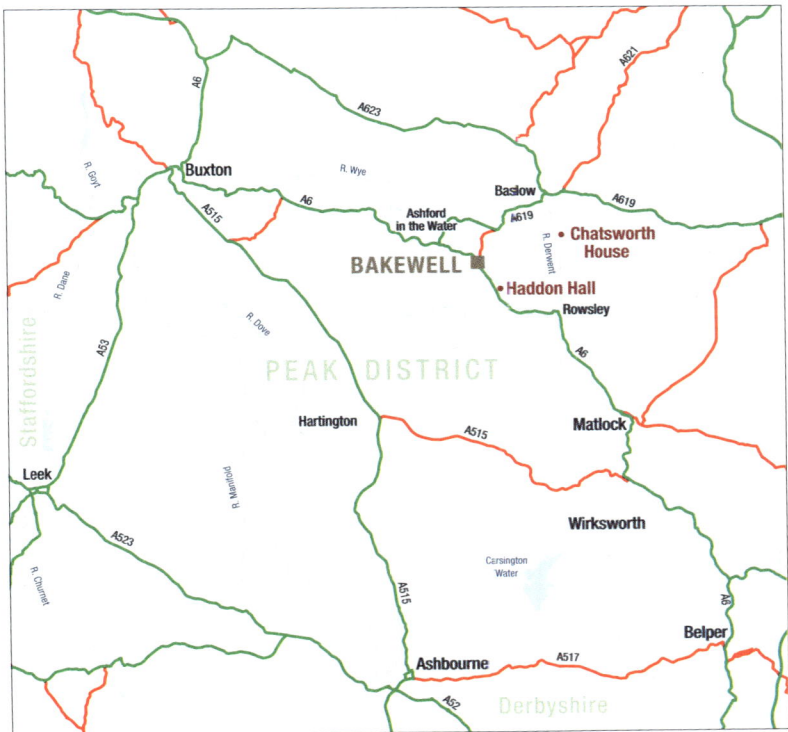

CURLEW
PRESS

Published by Curlew Press
Derbyshire

Email: mail@curlewpress.co.uk

British Library Cataloguing in Publication Data: a catalogue record for this book is available from the British Library.

1st Edition

ISBN: 978-1-7395500-1-1

FSC
www.fsc.org
MIX
Paper | Supporting
responsible forestry
FSC® C014540

Print – Short Run Press Ltd., Exeter, England
Text – Louise Maskill
Walks – Karl Barton
Editor – Louise Maskill
Design and layout – Mark Titterton

Photographs – Karl Barton – p.12, p.17, p.20 left, p.29 bottom, p.32, p.36 bottom right, p.40, p.58, p.60. Courtesy of Haddon Hall – p.51, p.52, p.53 and back cover.
Front cover and all other photography by Mark Titterton

Cover Photographs – front: Scot's Garden, Bakewell; **back left:** Chatsworth;
back right: Haddon Hall

Maps – © OpenStreetMap Contributors (openstreetmap.org). Contains OS data © Crown copyright and database right (2024)

Key to the maps in this book

······· Footpath	⎯⎯ Track/former route or road	🅸 Visitor information
●●●●● Walking route	┈┈┈ Railway	🅿 Parking
⎯⎯ Trunk road	⎯ ⎯ Tram line	**WC** Public toilets
⎯⎯ A road	⎯⎯ River	Grid: 1 mile square
⎯⎯ B road	Building	Contours: 10 metres
⎯⎯ Minor road	**Mill** Site of interest	Wood/plantation
⎯⎯ Service road		

Contents

A Souvenir and Walker's Guide to Bakewell, Chatsworth and Haddon

Chatsworth Park

Introduction

The triangle formed by the pretty market town of Bakewell and the nearby stately homes of Chatsworth House and Haddon Hall lies in Derbyshire on the eastern edge of the Peak District National Park. The surrounding countryside of gritstone edges and moorland interspersed by fertile dales is gentler than the craggy uplands of the Dark Peak further north, but no less rewarding to explore on foot. The landscape is criss-crossed by former turnpikes and rail lines, Roman roads, packhorse trails, and trade routes such as the ancient Portway, making for a varied and accessible walking experience.

Derbyshire is landlocked, but has a long connection with water. The county's industrial past is inextricably linked with its rivers and canals, as well as the water-powered textile mills that drove the Industrial Revolution, and the many geothermal springs that bubble to the surface have attracted health tourists to Derbyshire's spa resorts over millennia. The main towns of Derby, Buxton, Chesterfield and the Matlocks all have a long association with water, whether holy wells, thermal springs or transport links along rivers and canals, and many settlements in the region still celebrate their wells and water sources in the ancient annual tradition of well dressing.

Bakewell once had aspirations as a spa resort, but the reputation of its geothermal waters has been eclipsed in more recent years by its attraction as one of the major tourist centres in the Peak District. Visitors can take advantage of everything the town has to offer, but can also use it as a base to venture further afield. Chatsworth, the Palace of the Peak and home of the Duke of Devonshire, and Haddon Hall, owned by the Duke of Rutland, are both nearby, and are popular destinations.

Bakewell, Chatsworth and Haddon are all worthy of visits in their own right, but the twelve circular walks in this book will also take you off the beaten tourist track to explore the villages, dales and moors of this charming corner of the Peak District. The routes range in distance from 4 to 7½ miles and will take you to historic villages such as Baslow, Beeley, Rowsley and Stanton in Peak, offering snippets of fascinating local information along with the detailed walk instructions. You will also find more in-depth information about the town of Bakewell and the houses of Chatsworth and Haddon, in the hope that it will inspire you to explore them for yourself.

Bakewell

The town of Bakewell, the only market town within the Peak District National Park, lies on the River Wye some 25.5 miles from Derby, 10 miles from Matlock and 16 miles from Sheffield. The settlement is traceable back as far as 924, mentioned in the Anglo-Saxon Chronicle as *Baedeca's Waella* – the spring or well belonging to Baedeca. The Chronicle also suggests that Edward the Elder (son of Alfred the Great) had a fort in the area, of which there may be possible remains on Castlehill. Domesday in 1086 records Bakewell as *Badequella*, transforming into the modern form of the name over the intervening centuries.

The town has always relied on local agriculture and is still home to a thriving regular livestock market, as well as hosting one of the area's largest agricultural shows each summer. However, there is also a history of industry, with the remains of lead mines, quarries, brickworks and mills to be found locally. The Arkwright family, architects of the Industrial Revolution in Cromford some 11 miles to the south, had interests in Bakewell; they built Lumford Mill in 1777, powered by the waters of the Wye, although this was the cause of some dispute with the Dukes of Devonshire and Rutland who owned water rights upstream and downstream respectively. After the Arkwrights the mill was sold and resold, standing empty for a period and being damaged by fire in 1868, but it was still being used to spin cotton

Above: Scot's Garden, Bakewell

Right: Ancient carved stone fragments in the south porch of All Saints Church, Bakewell

Opposite page: The Rutland Arms, Bakewell

in 1898 when it was bought by a battery manufacturer. This operation closed in 1970, but Lumford Mill continues its industrial heritage; the site is now home to around 40 local businesses, some of which operate out of the old mill buildings.

Gritstone was quarried to the east of the town at Ball Cross Quarry, Wicksop Woods and Bakewell Edge, while limestone was extracted to the west at Stanage Edge and marble was quarried at Blackstone Hollow. There were deposits of chert, a hard sedimentary silicate rock, at Holme Bank and Pretoria Quarries, both of which were still active until the mid-20th century. Bakewell chert was of such good quality that it was preferred by Josiah Wedgewood (of Stoke Potteries fame) as an alternative to granite for grinding calcined flint, used as a whitening agent in pottery-making. The chert from Bakewell was originally carried by packhorse to the Staffordshire Potteries, until 1794 when it began to be shipped to Cromford for onward travel via the new Cromford Canal and more latterly by rail.

Bakewell's connection with the Vernon and later the Manners families, Earls and then Dukes of Rutland and lords of the manor, is recognised in a number of places around the town – perhaps most notably in the elegant Rutland Arms Hotel on The Square, but also in the Vernon Chapel in All Saints Church on King Street, which houses a number of family memorials, and in Lady Manners School which was endowed by Lady Grace Manners in 1637 and still bears her name. Other notable buildings in the town are Bath House, which is adjacent to Bath Gardens and was built by the Duke of Rutland, the Town Hall on King Street, built in 1709,

and the former Market Hall on Bridge Street. The bridge itself, spanning the River Wye with its five arches, was built around 1300 and widened in the 19th century.

All Saints Church is an impressive building, described by Pevsner as among the most ambitious in the county. It is 150 feet (46 metres) in length, cruciform, with crenellations and an octagonal tower and spire, and was built in many phases. The earliest parts date from the 12th century, with evidence of Norman construction in the west front and nave, but the shaft of an 8th century Anglian high cross in the graveyard and other fragments of Anglo-Saxon stonework built into the fabric of the building argue for much earlier occupation on the same site. A second early cross shaft, also in the churchyard and Anglo-Scandinavian in style, was brought to Bakewell from Two Dales after it was unearthed in a field in the 19th century. The south transept and chancel were added in the 13th century, and the tower was constructed in the 13th and 14th centuries and rebuilt in the 19th century. The living was given to the Dean and Chapter of Lichfield in 1192 by King John, and today is part of the Diocese of Derby.

Bakewell has been a magnet for tourists over many centuries. The town has two warm springs, one in the centre of town near Bath Gardens and the other, the Peat Well, at the far end of what is now the Recreation Ground on Haddon Road. At around 15°C they are not as warm as the springs in the rival resorts of Matlock and Matlock Bath, 10 miles to the southeast, and Buxton, 12 miles to the west, but nevertheless attempts were made to take advantage of the Georgian and Victorian passions for thermal bathing.

Left: The Old Original Bakewell Pudding Shop   **Right:** The 14th century bridge in Bakewell

Bath House, mentioned above, contains the remains of an elaborate bathing complex built by the Duke of Rutland, but he was unable to compete with the Duke of Devonshire's massive programme of investment in Buxton, and Bakewell Spa did not grow as rapidly or as successfully as its rivals.

However, it did start to attract increasing numbers of visitors, becoming known as a gateway to the outdoor pursuits to be found in the Peak District, and it retains that reputation today as a popular base for walkers, cyclists, climbers and others. As well as easy access to the local hills and dales, the High Peak and Tissington Trails are also close by, and the 8.5-mile Monsal Trail starts at the town's old railway station (which closed in 1967) and carries walkers and cyclists over the stunning Headstone Viaduct, offering glorious views over Monsal Dale and beyond.

Of course, it would be impossible to offer any account of Bakewell's history without mentioning the famous Bakewell Pudding (known elsewhere as Bakewell Tart, but make that mistake locally at your peril!). The real Bakewell Pudding, a rich confection of flaky pastry, jam, and almond and egg custard, is available at bakeries in the town, with the original recipe still a closely guarded secret. However, legend has it that the dish was created by accident when a kitchen maid working at the Old White Horse coaching inn, on the site of the present-day Rutland Arms Hotel, was instructed by the cook to make a strawberry tart. She misunderstood the directions, and instead of mixing the jam with the egg and almond custard, she spread it on the pastry and topped with the custard before baking. The result was an immediate success, and a local legend was born.

The following four walks, all starting and finishing in Bakewell, will take you around the town and as far afield as Ashford, along the Monsal Trail, and to Edensor and Chatsworth Park.

Walk 1: Bakewell Town Walk

Distance: 4½ miles   **Start:** Weir Bridge, Bakewell

ESSENTIAL INFORMATION

Bakewell

Public Transport: TM Travel 218 – Sheffield to Bakewell, via Chatsworth House; frequent daily service. **Trent Barton 6.1 Sixes** – Derby to Bakewell, via Matlock and Wirksworth; frequent daily service.
High Peak TP Transpeak – Buxton to Derby; frequent daily service.
Hulleys 170 – Chesterfield to Bakewell (170c via Chatsworth House); frequent daily service. **Hulleys 173** – Bakewell to Tideswell and Castleton; 2-hourly service Monday to Saturday. **Hulleys 257** – Sheffield to Bakewell; infrequent daily service. Hulleys also serve other local towns and villages via a number of routes to and through Bakewell.

Facilities: Public toilets may be found in Bakewell town centre – a small charge applies. Bakewell offers a multitude of shops, pubs, cafés, hotels and guest houses.

Car Park: Several car parks may be found in Bakewell. Fees apply.

About the Walk

This walk takes you on a journey along the streets and footpaths in Bakewell, highlighting a number of buildings of interest. Also venturing outside the urban landscape, we climb the side of the Derwent Valley to enjoy views over

Old House Museum, Bakewell

the town and pass the site of one of Derbyshire's lost medieval settlements. Returning to town beside the cemetery we follow the route of the former Grindleford Bridge to Newhaven turnpike, authorised in 1759. Ascending to the Old House Museum by way of the churchyard, we end our walk in the narrow lanes of the town centre.

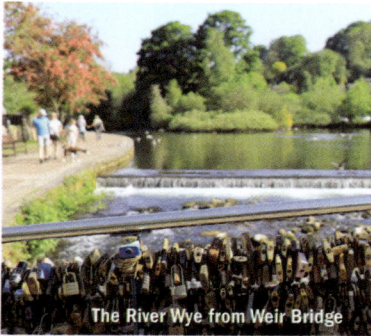

The River Wye from Weir Bridge

Directions

1. From Weir Bridge, follow the riverside walk beside the Wye, heading downstream for 100 yards to Granby Croft.

2. Keeping to the pavement of Granby Croft for a few yards, take the metalled path ahead, following the boundary of back gardens on your immediate right to enter Bakewell Recreation Ground.

3. Beyond the toilet block (seasonal), take the avenue bisecting the rec towards the rear of the houses along Wye Bank.

4. Beside the children's play area, continue ahead along the narrow path leading to Wye Bank. Beside the play area is Peat Well, one of the town's thermal springs which was referred to in a grant in the reign of Henry III.

5. Cross Wye Bank, taking the path opposite to pass between houses, gardens and allotments to Agricultural Way.

6. Cross Agricultural Way and turn right to reach Haddon Road, the A6.

7. Turn left along the A6 for 120 yards. This section of the A6 once formed part of the Wirksworth Moor to Longstone Turnpike.

8. Cross the busy A6 to Intake Lane. Follow the lane, which is initially metalled, as it winds its way uphill for around ¾ of a mile before coming to a gate across its path.

9. In the field beyond the gateway there is a stile is at 2 o'clock, if you are facing directly ahead and uphill. However, you should follow the public footpath as it continues uphill, following the wall line to your left. Continue almost to Youlgrave Road, then take the path that diverges to your right at 5 o'clock, taking you back down the hill to the stile you observed when entering the field. (The path that leads directly across the field to this point is unofficial.) The road at the top of the field is the conjectural route of the High Peak to Derby Roman Road and the Portway, later forming part of the Grindleford Bridge to Newhaven Turnpike of 1759.

10. Beyond the stile, the path cuts diagonally across a field and then continues in a similar direction across a much smaller field.

11. Descend over rough ground, which may be boggy, to a bridge over the stream. The lost medieval village of Burton is thought to have been located in this area.

12. Turning left to cross the bridge, continue uphill, initially with a wall line on your right. The path continues between walls before emerging in a field. To the

Holme Ln
A619
A6
Holme Bridge
River Wye
Scot's Garden
Buxton Rd.
Baslow Rd.
Station Rd.
Bakewell Bridge
Weir Bridge
START
Old House Museum
All Saints Church
Agricultural Business Centre
Granby Croft
Butts View
Matlock St
Agricultural Way
Peat Well
Haddon Rd
River Wye
Cemetery
Lost village of Burton
A6
WC
P
i
1
2
3
4
5
6
7
8
9
10
11
12
13
14
15
16
17
18
19
20
21
22
23
24
25
26
27
28
29
30
31
32
33
34
35
36
37
38
39
40

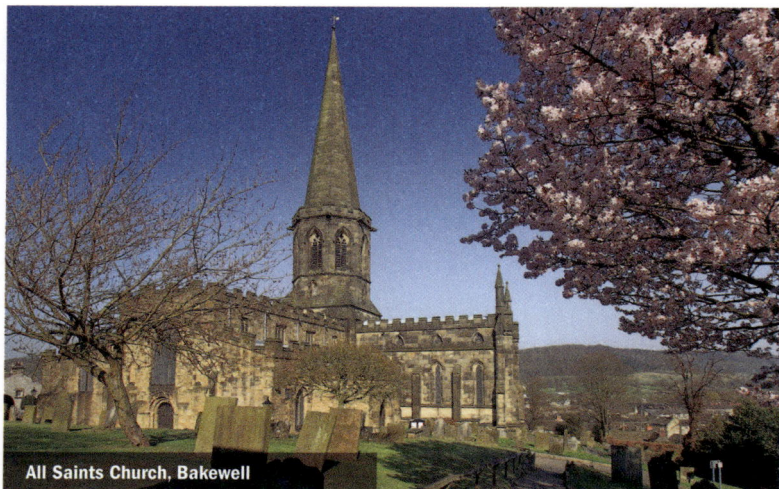

All Saints Church, Bakewell

right and downhill is Burton Closes Mews, with mid-19th century houses, a coach house and stables.

13. Continue ahead, keeping the wall line on your right.

14. Through the stile, follow the grassy lane for a few yards to a further gate and stile. Continue along this lane, with its surface becoming more even as it progresses, until you reach Burton Edge. On your right is the cemetery with its two chapels, both dating from 1858 but one Nonconformist and the other Church of England.

15. Keeping the cemetery on your right, follow Burton Edge to its junction with Upper Yeld Road.

16. Turn right for a few yards, with the entrance to the cemetery on your right. Upper Yeld Road becomes Calton View and Butts Road, and a public footpath descends to your right.

17. Take Butts Road on your right, and follow it downhill for around 200 yards.

18. Locate the wooden post and finger board of a public footpath sign, at the top of four concrete steps in the stone wall on your left. Follow the indicated earthen path to a squeezer stile at the end of Butts View.

19. Continue along Butts View to its junction with South Church Street.

20. Cross South Church Street and take the steps into the churchyard of All Saints Church, following the path uphill to the lych-gate and Church Lane. All Saints Church dates from the Norman period (the late 11th or early 12th century), but the churchyard contains the shafts of two much earlier crosses (both Grade I listed).

21. Turn right into Church Lane for 50 yards.

Saxon cross shaft, All Saints Churchyard

Holme Hall and Lumford House (left)

22. Take the footpath on your left, signposted "Museum".

23. From the top of the path, turn right in front of the Old House Museum and continue along Cunningham Place as it descends to a crossroads. The Old House Museum, formerly a parsonage dated 1543, is a probable reconstruction of an earlier building. Under lease from Philip Gell, the building was converted to tenements by Richard Arkwright in 1790. It was restored by the Bakewell Historical Society in 1959.

24. Cross Church Lane and descend Bagshaw Hill to Buxton Road (the A6).

25. Cross the busy A6 and turn left to follow the road for 250 yards. Progress Works, immediately on your left, was constructed as an inn alongside the diverted road, now the A6, for Arkwright in 1820.

26. Turn right onto the approach for Holme Bridge and the ford it stands beside. Cross the ancient packhorse bridge. Prior to the bridge on the left are the remains of a sheepwash, while Holme Bridge itself, a Grade I listed structure and scheduled monument, was built in 1684 to replace an earlier bridge. Opposite the bridge is Lumford House, formerly the home of Richard Arkwright.

27. Beyond the bridge, turn right into Holme Lane, which you follow for a little over 200 yards.

28. Take the path on your right over a water meadow. Do not take the path up to the roadside; instead, continue through the gate to Scot's Garden beyond, which in turn leads to Bakewell Bridge.

29. Ascend a couple of steps to Bridge Street. Facing the drinking fountain, Cross's Folly, turn right and cross the Wye via the narrow pavements of Bakewell Bridge.

Holme Hall

Holme Hall Chert Mine

Lumford House

27

Sheepwash

Holme Bridge

26

A6

Buxton Rd

Undercliffe

Mill leat

River Wye

Holme Ln

A619

Baslow Rd

28

Scot's Garden

Victoria Mill

S. Anselm's School

Milford House

Mill leat

32

Milford Bridge

31

Castle St

25

Bagshaw Hill

Bagshaw Hall

33

30

29 Cross's Folly

Bakewell Bridge

The Woodyard

24

34

Bath St.

Bath House

Bath Gardens

Rutland St.

Market Hall

39 40

Market St.

Weir Bridge

Old House Museum

23

22

All Saints Church

Cross

21

20

Rutland Arms

35

36

Water St.

38

WC

37

1 START

B5055

Mallock St.

Granby Rd.

P

2

Butts View

19

Granby Croft

River Wye

18

Haddon Rd

3

West Lodge, Holme Lane

30. Beyond the bridge, turn right and walk along the first section of Castle Street to Milford Bridge. This dates from the late 18th or early 19th century, and crosses the tail race from Victoria Mill.

31. Prior to the bridge, bear left to take the path, Brookside, for 50 yards.

32. Turn left along a footpath, which leads to New Street and its junction with Bath Street.

33. Turn right into Bath Street, following the road around to the right.

34. Opposite the infant school, turn right into Bath Gardens and follow the path through to Rutland Square. Bath House was built in 1697 and housed one of Bakewell's warm springs; a well now stands in the memorial garden to one side of the property.

35. Cross the busy road and take Water Street opposite.

36. Immediately turn right into Diamond Court, then follow the path as it makes its way between buildings to make a sharp left turn past the swimming bath and Orm Court beyond.

37. Turn left into Granby Road, and after only a few yards turn left again into Water Street, which you follow for 50 yards to its junction with Water Lane.

38. Follow Water Lane to its junction with Bridge Street.

39. Turn right into Bridge Street, walking the short distance to the Tourist Information Centre which is housed in the 17th century former Market Hall.

40. Turn right crossing the car park to Market Street where you turn right. After a few yards your starting point at Weir Bridge will be visible on your left.

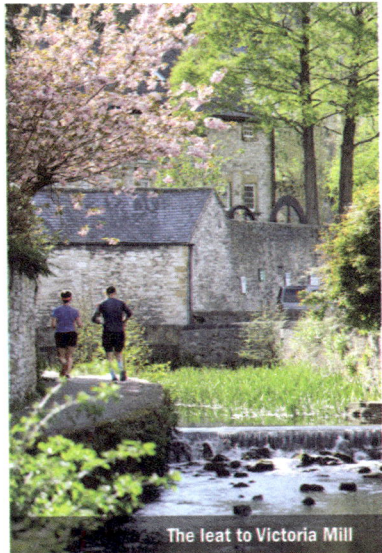

The leat to Victoria Mill

Sheepwash Bridge, Ashford in the Water

Walk 2: Bakewell and Ashford in the Water

Distance: 6 miles   **Start:** Weir Bridge, Bakewell

ESSENTIAL INFORMATION

Public Transport: As well as those previously listed for Bakewell, the following buses also serve Ashford: **High Peak TP Transpeak** – Buxton to Derby; frequent daily service. **Hulleys 173** – Bakewell to Tideswell and Castleton; two-hourly service Monday to Saturday.

Facilities: A shop, pub, hotel and guest houses can be found in Ashford. Ashford toilets, small charge via honesty box; see local signs.

Car Park: Several car parks may be found in Bakewell. Fees apply. Parking in Ashford, payment via honesty box; see local signs.

About the Walk

Starting this walk in the centre of Bakewell, we make our way alongside a mill leat towards Victoria Mill before climbing steeply to pass S. Anselm's school and then descending to the side of the River Wye, noting the evidence of its previous use to provide power for the mills downstream. As we near Ashford in the Water further signs of water management may be observed beside the former Wirksworth Moor to Longstone turnpike, now a quiet lane. Passing through the picturesque village of Ashford, we make a short diversion to view its packhorse bridge and adjacent sheepwash. Ascending to higher ground once more, we take advantage of another long-forgotten turnpike before returning to Bakewell, passing close by the entrance to an abandoned chert mine.

Note: The road crossing beyond Ashford is at a point with poor visibility, and the 50 mph speed limit is often exceeded. Please take care here.

Directions

1. From Weir Bridge turn right into Market Street, following it the short distance to Bridge Street.

2. Cross Bridge Street and take the public footpath between buildings to the right of the Wheatsheaf public house.

3. Emerging on Bath Street, cross the road and continue ahead up New Street, which soon becomes a public footpath taking you to Brookside.

4. Turn left into Brookside, following the mill leat upstream to Victoria Mill and Mill Street. To your left is the 18th century Milford House, and to the right is a bridge over Victoria Mill's tail race. Note the obelisk attached to the downstream

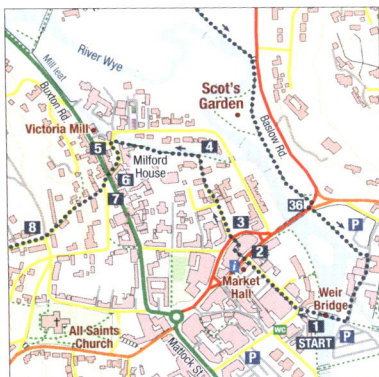

parapet. According to census information, for several decades around the end of the 19th century Milford House was the residence of the retired cotton spinner Robert Cross, the son of a Blackburn banker named James Cross. Ahead is the 18th century Victoria Mill, the latest of several mills on or around this site. It originally boasted a 16-foot breast shot waterwheel with a width of 13½ feet.

5. Turn left into Mill Street, following the road as it curves to the right and meets Buxton Road.

6. Cross Buxton Road and ascend Bagshaw Hill for around 30 yards.

Victoria Mill

7. Turn right into the steep Fly Hill, continuing upwards as the path becomes a road heading towards Stanedge Road.

8. Go straight ahead at Stanedge Road, following it as it makes a 90° turn to the right. Pass the houses, buildings and car park entrances of S. Anselm's prep school.

9. Immediately beyond the second entrance to the school car park, take the public footpath on your right. (Note that this path has been redirected, and its current location is not shown on Ordnance Survey maps or Derbyshire County Council's definitive map.) Follow the path between school playing fields before entering Endcliff Wood. The path descends steeply, emerging on Buxton Road. Chert mining was once carried out in the vicinity of Endcliff Wood, presumably for use in the ceramics industry, with the product therefore probably being transported to the Staffordshire Potteries.

10. Cross Buxton Road and turn left for a few yards.

11. Turn right onto a public footpath across a field, heading towards the small Lakeside housing estate.

12. Cross Lakeside and take the footpath immediately opposite. Beyond the houses, follow the path across fields, known as Gay Pastures, with views over the Wye Valley and its water management features on your right. Continue along the path as it descends and then ascends again close to a weir across the River Wye and Ashford Lake, before descending once more to the Wye, or one of its mill leats. The water management features in this valley were constructed to power Sir Richard Arkwright's Lumford Mill, for which he leased the land from his extended family member and local bigwig Philip Gell, who lived at Hopton around 10 miles away as the crow flies. Lumford Mill was the third of Arkwright's mills in Derbyshire, constructed in 1777, later managed by his son Richard Arkwright, and rebuilt in 1868 following a catastrophic fire.

13. Turn right onto Buxton Road and almost immediately right again onto the now quiet Mill Lane that leads into the village of Ashford, crossing Lees Bridge and Mill Bridge. Mill Lane follows the route of the Wirksworth Moor to Longstone turnpike of 1759, and lies on the conjectural path of the Portway. Lees Bridge is contemporary with the turnpike and possibly the flour mill a little way upstream, since it crosses the mill's leat, while Mill Bridge bears a stone with the inscription 'M HYDE 1664'. Legend has it that Mr Hyde was the local vicar, or perhaps just a hapless traveller, who was thrown from his horse and fell from the bridge, sadly drowning in the river beneath.

14. Cross the A6020 into Greaves Lane.

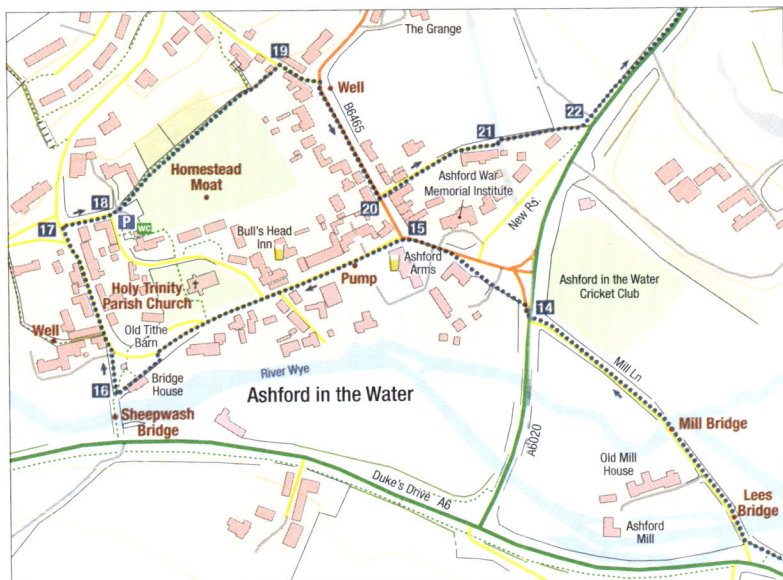

Ashford in the Water

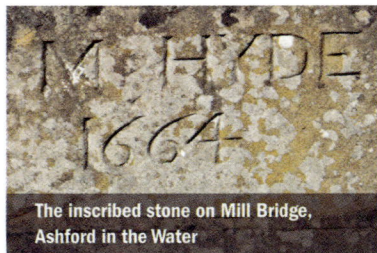

The inscribed stone on Mill Bridge, Ashford in the Water

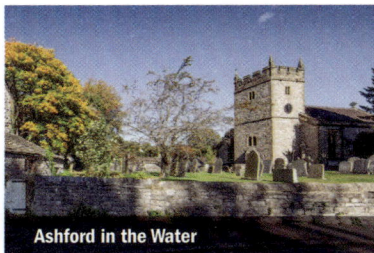

Ashford in the Water

15. Turn left into Church Street by the Ashford Arms Hotel. Pass the village pump on your left, the shop and the Bulls Head pub on your right, as far as a shelter and the junction with Fennel Street.

On your left, and well worth a visit, is the 16th century Sheepwash Bridge, an ancient packhorse bridge over the Wye. As its name suggests, an associated enclosure was used in the process of herding sheep into the river for a wash. The bridge was extended in the 18th century and continued in use as part of the Longnor to Rowland turnpike of 1765.

16. Continue up Fennel Street to another shelter and the junction with Buxton Road, Vicarage Lane and Court Lane.

17. Turn right into Court Lane for a few yards.

18. Continue ahead into Hall Orchard playing field, taking the metalled footpath beside a wall which forms the leftmost boundary. Continue along the path as it squeezes between a hedge and a wall. Within the playing field lie the remains of Homestead Moat, believed to be all that is left of a medieval moated residence associated with the Neville family.

19. Turn right into Hill Cross, and after only a few yards turn right again into Greaves Lane, following it for 100 yards. Opposite the junction with Hill Cross is the remains of the village pump. Sadly the iron pump itself is no longer present, having disappeared sometime since the early 1980s, but together with other water sources around the village the site is decorated during the annual well dressings.

20. Turn left into Hall End Lane, following the road for 100 yards, noting a stream passing beneath an arch in a drystone wall to your left. Hall End Lane once formed part of the Longnor to Rowland turnpike, which continued to the right and made its way past the front of Ashford Hall, which the road predates by around 20 years.

21. Immediately beyond the stream, pass through the stile on your left and continue to the A6020.

22. Turn left and follow the A6020 for around 275 yards. This section of road formed part of the Chesterfield to Ashford turnpike of 1812, which effectively diverted the Longnor turnpike away from Ashford Hall.

23. Cross the busy road to pass through a stile and descend a short distance to cross a stream, before making your ascent through the wood.

24. Emerging from the wood, cross a stile and continue your ascent ahead. To your left are views of Thornbridge Hall and Longstone Edge beyond.

25. Cross a stone stepped stile over a wall. With Churchdale Hall on your left, continue over the field towards a metalled lane.

26. Cross the stile with its adjacent fingerpost directing you to the left, and follow the lane past the drive to Churchdale Hall, Churchdale Farm and Churchdale Cottage before reaching the A6020 once again. The lane along which you just walked was the original line of the Longnor to Rowland turnpike, the route of which was diverted by the construction of the Midland Railway.

27. Turn right onto the A6020 for 300 yards.

28. Opposite the 17th century Rowdale House, take the footpath across a field on your right.

29. Enter Cracknowl Wood via a pedestrian gate and ascend to fields beyond.

30. Cross the stile at the top of the wood and follow the path across fields.

31. Through a pedestrian gate close to Cracknowl Farm on your right, continue uphill to a pedestrian gate in the wall to your left. As you crest the hill, enjoy the views over Bakewell.

32. Pass through the gate, crossing an initially pockmarked field to a pedestrian gate close to the far corner of the enclosure.

33. Turn right down the path from Hassop, which becomes Holme Bank as it descends past two former chert quarries and the abandoned Holme Hall chert mine and its associated remaining infrastructure. A so known as Bakewell (Smith's) mine, 8 known entrances exist in the surrounding area, including a gated portal on your left. Holme Hall, also on your left, has a date stone of 1626 incorporated into its façade, with some parts of the building dating from the 14th or 15th century. The hall is surrounded by manicured gardens containing a 17th century gazebo.

34. At the bottom of the hill, turn left into Holme Lane for 200 yards. To your right at the bottom of Holme Bank is Lumford House, the former residence of Richard Arkwright whose mill you passed earlier in the walk.

35. Take the path on your right over the meadow, following it into Scot's Garden and ultimately Baslow Road/ Bridge Street opposite Cross's Folly. This drinking fountain was built in 1876 to commemorate the provision of a piped water supply from Coombes Hill to every house in Bakewell.

36. Cross the road and take the path opposite, which returns you to Weir Bridge.

Walk 3: Bakewell and the Monsal Trail

Distance: 4 miles **Start:** Bakewell Bridge, Bakewell

ESSENTIAL INFORMATION

Facilities: The former Hassop Station offers a large cafe (also offering takeaway food), cycle hire and bed and breakfast accommodation.

About the Walk

From the 14th century Bakewell Bridge we cross Scot's Garden to pass the former residence of Richard Arkwright Jr., the son of the industrial pioneer of the same name, who followed in the family business of exploiting the power of water in the manufacture of textiles. We climb steeply to pass Holme Hall and the chert mine named after it. Following an ancient walled former packhorse way as it threads its way across the high pastures, we reach the trackbed of the Midland Railway which once carried express trains between London and Manchester. We return to Bakewell via the Monsal Trail.

Directions

1. From Bakewell Bridge, take the footpath across Scot's Garden to Holme Lane.

2. Once through the pedestrian gate, turn left into Holme Lane and continue for around 200 yards.

3. Turn right beside Lumford House, which is adorned by a blue plaque recording the building as the former residence of Richard Arkwright Jr. and his involvement with the nearby Lumford Mill. Keep to the lane, the surface of which changes from metalled to a dirt track as you ascend past the remains of Holme Hall chert mine and Holme Hall, both on your right.

Cross's Folly fountain. The footpath into Scot's Garden is through the gate on the opposite side of the road

5 Former Midland Main Line - Monsal Trail

A6020

A6020

Former Hassop
Railway Station

P

Hassop Rd
B6001

Former Midland Main Line - Monsal Trail

4

Quarry

Holme Hall
Chert Mine

Quarry

Holme
Hall

2 Holme Ln

Lumford
House **3**

Holme
Bridge

Baslow Rd.

B6001

6

P

7

Former Bakewell
Railway Station

A6

Scot's
Garden

Cross's
Folly

Castle Hill

B6408

River Wye

Station Rd.

1

START

Bakewell
Bridge

P

P

4. Beside a dew pond on your left, continue ahead through the gate into a walled track. Follow the track as it ascends and descends for just short of a mile towards the Monsal Trail, passing through several gates.

5. Once on the Monsal Trail, turn right to follow the trail past the former Hassop Station to the former Bakewell Station 1¼ miles away.

6. Turn right beside the former station building, emerging in a car park. Walk through the car park to Station Road.

7. Turn left into Station Road and keep right as Handley Lane joins from the left. Follow Station Road down to Bakewell Bridge around a quarter of a mile away.

The former Hassop Station on the Monsal Trail, which offers cycle hire, a gift shop and a café

Walk 4: Bakewell, Edensor and Chatsworth

Distance: 7½ miles   **Start:** Bakewell Bridge, Bakewell

ESSENTIAL INFORMATION

Public Transport: As well as those previously listed for Bakewell, the following buses also serve Chatsworth House:
Stagecoach Peak Sightseer (open top bus) – Bakewell to Chatsworth House loop; seasonal. **TM Travel 218** – Sheffield to Bakewell, via Chatsworth House; frequent daily service. **Hulleys 170** – Chesterfield to Bakewell (170c via Chatsworth House); frequent daily service.

Facilities: Edensor Tea Cottage provides all you would expect from a traditional tea room. Chatsworth House, a short diversion from the route of this walk, offers numerous shops, food outlets and toilets in the former stable block. Chatsworth Garden Centre at Calton Lees contains a café. Holiday accommodation may be found across the Chatsworth Estate.

Car Park: Additionally at Chatsworth House and Calton Lees. Fees apply.

About the Walk

Between Bakewell and Edensor we follow the route of a former packhorse way, passing a guide stoop at Ball Cross advertising routes to Bakewell, Chesterfield and Sheffield. We continue along the Chesterfield way down to the village of Edensor (pronounced *Enza*), which was once located closer to Chatsworth House but was moved to its present

Edensor village

location during landscaping work on the estate, in order for the Dukes of Devonshire to have a more pleasing view across the valley. Making our way across the parkland of the Chatsworth Estate we pass by the location of the original mill and packhorse bridge. Our return to Bakewell, via Calton Lees and Calton Pastures, takes us close to a number of estate buildings, some of which may be rented as holiday accommodation.

Directions

1. From the drinking fountain at Bakewell Bridge, climb Station Road to its junction with Handley Lane, adjacent to the former railway station.

2. Bear right up Station Road, crossing the former Midland Main Line (now the Monsal Trail) via a stone bridge.

3. A few yards beyond Stationmaster's House take the bridleway on your right, which you follow for around ⅓ of a mile up a steep gradient along a deeply rutted path. Continue without deviation as you cross a golf course, other lanes and paths. A bell is provided for your safety, alerting any golfers to your presence.

4. Turn right into Handley Lane at Ballcross and follow the lane for approximately ½ a mile as it initially ascends and then descends towards Pilsley and Edensor.

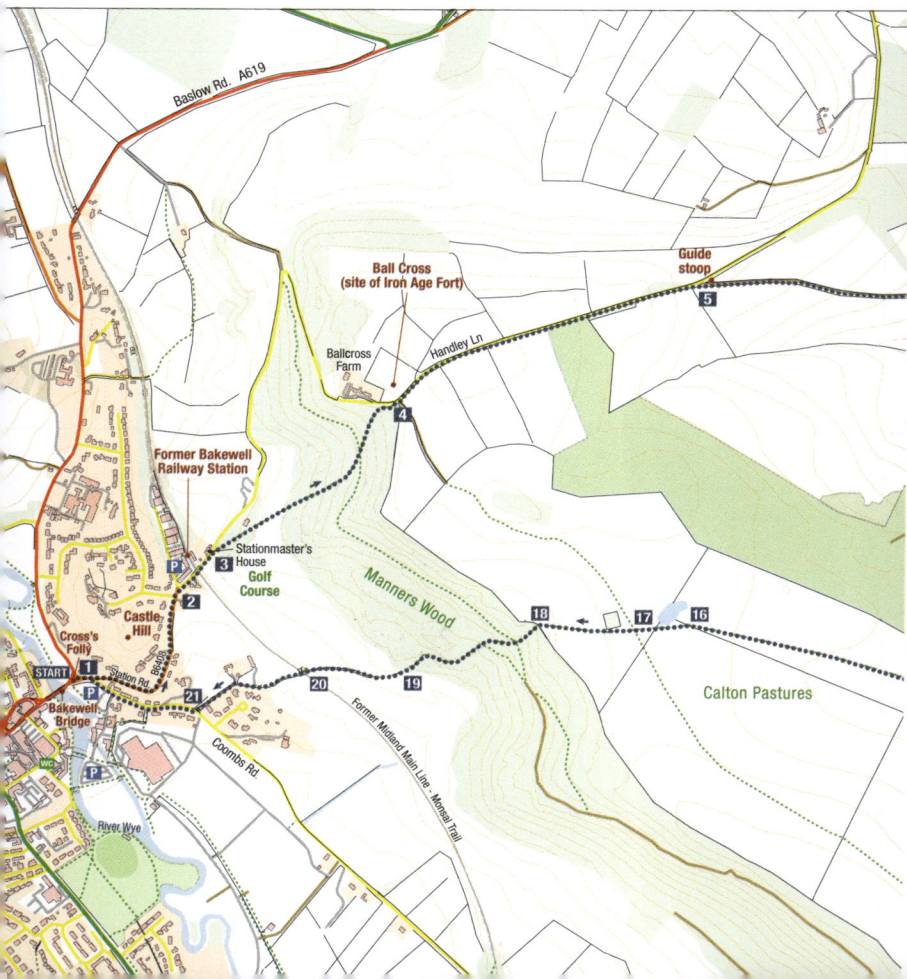

5. At the fork in the road, take the less well made track on your right. Continue down the lane for about a mile to Edensor in the Derwent Valley. On your left, immediately after taking the right-hand fork is a guide stoop, a stone marker erected in the 18th century to assist navigation across the sparsely populated uplands of Derbyshire. The stone is inscribed with directions to Bakewell, Chesterfield and Sheffield, and the date 1709.

6. Once through the village of Edensor, take the pedestrian turnstile beside the cattle grid and cross the B6012, which can be extremely busy with fast-moving traffic. Follow the white gravelled path opposite to its end at Paine's Bridge. The house to the right of the path is the only surviving cottage from the original village of Edensor.

7. Cross the driveway to Chatsworth House prior to the bridge. This access

St Peter's Church, Edensor

road to Chatsworth House can become very busy. If you wish to visit Chatsworth House, cross the bridge to explore everything the house has to offer. Otherwise, bear right to follow the public footpath across grazed parkland to the B6012 around a mile away, close to a cattle grid and the entrance to Calton Lees, Chatsworth Garden Centre and car park.

8. Cross the B6012 and turn left, shortly passing through a pedestrian gate beside its larger equestrian sibling and cattle grid.

9. Beyond the gate, follow the path towards the car park, and then follow the road towards the garden centre.

10. Passing the garden centre on your left, continue along the metalled lane as it turns to the right. 150 yards beyond the tradesman's entrance to the garden centre you reach a crossing of lanes, with the hamlet of Calton Lees behind you and to the left.

11. Continue ahead for around ¾ of a mile, following the sign for Rye Croft and Pingle Cottage, noted on the OS map as Calton Houses. As you follow the lane, which lies alongside a stream, you will see a spring and a stone trough on your right.

12. After ascending the steep hairpins which lead to the Calton Houses, take the lane which continues between the dwellings, reaching a gate after 100 yards or so leading back into the managed parkland.

13. Follow the path ahead for just shy of 200 yards, keeping the wall line on your immediate right.

14. Once through the large pedestrian gate, follow the path to its intersection with a wide grassy track, with the Russian Cottage some 250 yards away to your right.

15. Turn left onto the wide grass track and cross the meadow, passing a gateway after around ⅓ of a mile to reach a mere after a further ⅓ of a mile.

16. Take the pedestrian gate and skirt the mere on your right to a further pedestrian gate.

17. Follow the path across pasture, with a copse on your right, down to the margin of the woods beyond.

18. A pedestrian gate guards the entrance to Manners Wood and the challenging

path that descends to Bakewell golf course. The path is steep in places with a rough and rutted surface. Follow the path through the wood, ignoring any paths that cross your track.

19. Cross the golf course, giving the bell a good ring as you pass, and follow the path, now between fences, as it descends to the former Midland Main Line.

20. If you wish to return to Bakewell Station, take the steps on your right to descend to the former track level and turn right for a short walk up the Monsal Trail. Otherwise, continue over the bridge, negotiating a gate into a field to descend to a farm track, which you follow to the left down to Coombs Road.

21. Turn right onto Coombs Road and follow it for 250 yards to its junction with Station Road, from where you can see the drinking fountain and Bakewell Bridge on your left.

The Russian Cottage, near Calton Lees

Chatsworth

Chatsworth House, the Palace of the Peak, has been home to the Cavendish family since Tudor times, being acquired by Sir William Cavendish in the mid-16th century. Sir William was the second husband of the formidable Bess of Hardwick, and in 1553 they commenced construction of an Elizabethan manor house near the site of an earlier residence.

Although Bess married twice more after Sir William's death in 1557, Chatsworth remained in the Cavendish family via their sons. Bess and her fourth husband, George Talbot, 6th Earl of Shrewsbury, were custodians of Mary, Queen of Scots during her twenty-year captivity at the hands of Elizabeth I, and Mary was kept at Chatsworth for periods of time between 1569 and 1584.

In 1684 the house was inherited by Bess and William's grandson, also William, 4th Earl of Devonshire, who became the 1st Duke in 1694. He remodelled the Elizabethan house, creating the south, east and west façades and laying out formal gardens, the Canal Pond and the Cascade. In the 1760s the 4th Duke added a bridge, stables and a kitchen and office wing, and employed Capability Brown to enhance the estate's parkland; the winding approach to the house was created at this time, and the village of Edensor was moved because its old site was in view from the house.

Another of Chatsworth's famous residents was Georgiana, wife of the 5th Duke and Duchess of Devonshire from 1774 to her death in 1806. Georgiana was a celebrated socialite, and she filled Chatsworth with writers, politicians and artists. Her son the 6th Duke (known as the Bachelor Duke) continued Georgiana's tradition of lavish entertainment as well as improving the house and gardens; from 1815 onwards he employed Sir Jeffry Wyatville to create a library from the old Long Gallery and add the palatial new North Wing. He also appointed Joseph Paxton to create formal gardens, structures such as a Great Conservatory (now demolished; the maze stands on its former site), giant rockeries, and the gravity-fed Emperor Fountain in the Canal Pond, which could rise to over 280 feet (85 metres) on a calm day. The 6th Duke was also responsible for massive investment in the town of Buxton, developing it into a spa resort to rival Bath and Harrogate; see *The Spa Waters of Derbyshire*, also published by Curlew, for more about this fascinating aspect of Derbyshire's social history.

Chatsworth was developed into the attraction it is today largely by the 11th Duke, Andrew Cavendish, and his wife Deborah. They succeeded to the title in 1950, but were hit by ruinous death duties and had to make the

Chatsworth House

estate pay for itself. They modernised the house and its facilities, creating a farm shop, catering outlets, a farmyard, adventure playground and retail shops. The 11th Duke died in 2006 and was succeeded by his son Peregrine, known as Stoker. Along with his wife Amanda, the 12th Duke has continued to develop Chatsworth as a family home, a tourist magnet and a venue for the arts, hosting temporary sculpture exhibitions in the house and gardens.

Within the house itself, the Painted Hall is the largest and grandest room, occupying the same position as the Elizabethan Great Hall. It has been remodelled over the years, but the masterful painted panels by Louis Laguerre depicting the life of Julius Caesar date back to the room's creation in 1687–1694. Also of particular interest is the Chapel, one of the glories of Chatsworth, which has remained almost unaltered since it was built between 1688 and 1693. The altarpiece was carved from alabaster and Ashford black marble by the master craftsman Samuel Watson, whose carvings can also be seen elsewhere in the house. Among many other works of art and architectural features, look out for the wood carvings in the Oak Room and State Apartments, and items from the 12th Duke's extensive art and sculpture collection throughout.

Chatsworth House and Gardens

Outdoors, the gardens are a day out in themselves, offering over 100 acres (40.5 hectares) of carefully tended lawns, fountains, cascades, sculptures, rockeries, greenhouses, a maze and an arboretum, all connected by magnificent drives and pathways. The wider park covers 990 acres (400 hectares), and is enclosed by a 9-mile (14.5 km) stone wall to contain the sheep, cattle and deer that roam the estate. The majority of it is open to the public, the exception being a Site of Special Scientific Interest known as the Old Park, a unique habitat containing nearly 400 veteran trees (over 500 years old) and offering a sanctuary to invertebrates, fungi and other flora and fauna. During the year the park is a venue for outdoor and countryside events such as concerts, horse trials and the famous Chatsworth Country Fair every autumn.

The walks that follow will take you on a tour of Chatsworth's stunning environs. You will explore the landscaped park and the village of Edensor, as well as heading further afield to the villages of Curbar, Baslow, Pilsley and Rowsley. None of the walks require entry to the House or Gardens, but you are heartily recommended to set aside time (perhaps even a full day!) for this as well.

Walk 5: Baslow, Chatsworth and Robin Hood

Distance: 7 miles   **Start:** The car park at Nether End in Baslow

ESSENTIAL INFORMATION

Public Transport: As well as the buses serving Baslow, the following services also call at Chatsworth House:
TM Travel 218 – Sheffield to Bakewell, via Chatsworth House; frequent daily service. **Hulleys 170** – Chesterfield to Bakewell (170c via Chatsworth House); frequent daily service. **High Peak 58** – operates twice daily in each direction on Sundays and Bank Holidays, between Macclesfield, Buxton, Monyash, Bakewell and Chatsworth House. The following services also call at Robin Hood:
Hulleys 170 – Chesterfield to Bakewell (170c via Chatsworth House); frequent daily service.

Facilities: As well as the amenities to be found in Baslow, Chatsworth House, a short distance from the route of this walk, offers numerous shops, food outlets and toilets in the former stable block. The Robin Hood public house is only a few yards from this walk.

Car Park: As well as the parking in Baslow, there are also car parks at Chatsworth House and Robin Hood public house. Fees apply.

About the Walk

From Nether End car park we head along a short section of the Eastmoor to Wardlow turnpike of 1759, crossing its bridge over Bar Brook. Walking across the landscaped parkland towards Chatsworth House we pass close by the lost settlement of Langley (a field of the same name was noted in the area on Senior's map of 1617) and a former ice house, now a horse jump. Approaching Chatsworth House we come to the imposing former stables, built between 1758 and 1763 and now housing shops, cafés and toilets. Climbing steeply through Stand Wood we reach the Hunting Tower, also known as the Stand. Built in the early 1580s, this is one of the few surviving structures contemporary with the previous iteration of Chatsworth House, and it offers outstanding views over the Derwent Valley.

Above Dobb Edge we pass a cup and ring stone, a fine example of prehistoric rock art which was exposed following erosion in 2012. Below Dobb Edge and the area known as Jumble Hole there is evidence of millstone manufacture. Descending to Heathy Lea Brook,

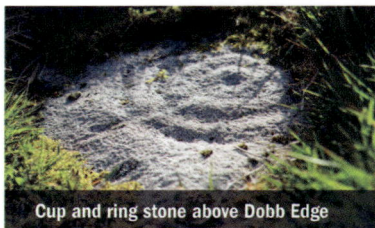

Cup and ring stone above Dobb Edge

we cross the route of the Eastmoor to Wardlow turnpike before rising to the current A619, formerly the Chesterfield to Hernstone Lane Head turnpike of 1769, rerouted over Eastmoor in 1830. Evidence of coal mining in the form of bell pits is to be found in the area around Robin Hood, and we pass a cairnfield, ring barrow and long house between Robin Hood and Cat Stones.

Descending back towards Bar Brook we pass through the former industrial landscape beneath Gardom's Edge, with quarries and evidence of millstone manufacture. Crossing the former Baslow to Owler Bar turnpike of 1803, now the A621, we pass close to a former slag mill, a cupola furnace, the site of a toll bar and a packhorse bridge over Bar Brook. Rising back up towards Blackstone Edge we enter another site where millstones were once manufactured. Returning to Baslow via Bar Road, a former packhorse way, we pass Lady Wall Well on Black Bank.

Directions

1. Starting from the Nether End area of Baslow, put your back to the toilet block and turn right along Church Lane, crossing Bar Brook after around 80 yards.

2. Just beyond the bridge over Bar Brook, turn right along a metalled lane for 300 yards, passing Plantation Cottage as the lane veers to the left.

3. Pass through the turnstile to enter Chatsworth Park, and take the left-hand path which leads to a metalled drive.

4. Turn right and follow the roadway through Chatsworth Park for around ¾ of a mile.

5. Take the left-hand fork towards the car parks, which you cut through to reach the stable block.

6. Facing Stand Wood, with the stable block on your right, follow the metalled lane beyond a sign for the "Farmyard and Adventure Playground" to a pair of gates.

7. 50 yards beyond the left-hand gate, on your right is a pedestrian gate through which you should pass. Cross the metalled lane to a dirt path opposite, which you follow for 65 yards uphill.

8. With the "stockyard" on your right, join the lane which merges on your left and continue ahead for a further 60 odd yards to a track on your left.

Wellington's Monument

24

Packhorse bridge

22

23

Ruined slag mill

21

Former toll house

25

Gardom's Edge

Sheffield Rd. A621

Birchen Edge

orse Bank Farm

Lady Wall Well

Bar Rd.

Over End

26

Site of Baslow Hydro

20

Cat Stones

Moorside Farm

Baslow

Eaton Hill

A619

Ring cairn

The Robin Hood Inn

Coal field

START

1

Nether End

A619

19

17

18

2

Former saw mill

Heathy Lea Brook

Baslow Village Hall

P WC

3

Jumble Coppice

16

4

Dobb Edge

15

Cup and ring engraved stone

14

13

White Lodge

Derwent Aqueduct (DVWB)

Lost village of Langley

Original course of Derwent

12

Hunting Tower

11

5

6

7

8

10

Queen Mary's Bower

P

9

Stable Block

River Derwent

WC

Paine's Bridge

Chatsworth House

Left: The Hunting Tower **Top right:** View from Dobb Edge **Bottom right:** Wellington Monument

9. Following the three footpath markers, turn left up the track for 70 yards and an intersection of tracks and path.

10. Take the path opposite, which will soon become a winding flight of steps taking you up to the lane that skirts the Hunting Tower.

11. Ahead is a further flight of steps leading to the tower and its grounds, affording views over the Derwent Valley. However, our route takes us left along the lane, circumnavigating the tower for 30 yards and then taking the lane to the left, continuing our journey around the tower for 120 yards.

12. Turn left and follow the woodland track without deviation for around ½ a mile.

13. A couple of yards shy of a five-barred gate blocking your path, turn left, walking a short distance to a stile over the wall.

14. Once over the stile, follow the path through the bracken field alongside the wall to your right, with Dobb Edge on your left. Continue for a little over 400 yards, where the path heads away from the wall on your right to steps set into the six-foot wall ahead.

15. On the other side of the stile, continue through the field for around 270 yards. To your left are views towards Baslow down the valley of Heathy Lea Brook.

16. Crossing the field boundary into bracken and a lightly wooded area, continue for a little under ½ a mile down to Heathy Lea Brook. The path meanders in and out of the bracken, crossing into a field for a short distance and several times coming within inches of a precipitous drop to your left into a more densely wooded area, before descending to a relatively flat and grassy area prior to the brook.

17. Cross the bridge over Heathy Lea brook and ascend a short flight of steps to the roadside by the A619.

18. Cross the busy road. The Robin Hood Inn is a short distance to your right, but our next waypoint is 50 yards to the left.

19. Turn right over the stone stepped stile, signed by a broken cast metal finger board proclaiming "PUBLIC FOOT" on one side. Follow this broad path uphill and away from the road, through the bracken and rock-strewn landscape. After around 500 yards, with Cat Stones ahead, you reach the crossing of a long-forgotten path leading from Moorside Farm on your right. The area of the intersection is marked as an "enclosure" on modern OS maps, but according to the Historic Environment Record the outline is all that remains of a ring cairn. Continue past Cat Stones on your right to a gate and stile in the wall ahead, offering views up the Derwent Valley.

20. For the next 1,000 yards the path descends fairly gently down to Sheffield Road (the A621), passing through woodland and crossing the ghosts of former quarry tracks and trade routes, with Gardom's Edge ever present on your right.

21. Cross the busy Sheffield Road to the footpath almost opposite, which immediately turns to the right and descends beside Barbrook Slag Mill. A cupola furnace was once sited on the opposite side of the road a few yards towards Baslow, as was the toll house for the Sheffield to Baslow turnpike.

22. Cross the packhorse bridge over Bar Brook to begin the steep ascent towards Wellington's Monument. Take the rough steps to the left of a metal railing.

23. At the stone stoop set into the corner of a boundary wall, turn right and initially follow the wall line on your left. The course of the path may be a little indistinct, but the wall on your left is never more than 30 yards away.

24. Continue to follow the wall line as it makes a sharp turn to the left and your ascent becomes more gentle. After 140 yards Wellington's Monument is 60 foot above you, to your right. Continue for around ¼ of a mile to reach the rough track named Bar Road.

25. Turn left and pass through the equestrian gate to follow Bar Road for around ¾ of a mile as it snakes its way down to Eaton Hill, crossing over the Derwent Aqueduct and alongside the former grounds of Baslow's Grand Hotel and Hydro as you go.

26. Turn left down Eaton Hill for 430 yards, using a pedestrian crossing to ease your passage across the busy Cock Hill (A619) to reach your final destination.

Walk 6: Baslow, Chatsworth, Edensor and Pilsley

Distance: 6 miles   **Start:** The car park at Nether End in Baslow

ESSENTIAL INFORMATION

Public Transport: As well as buses serving Baslow, the following services also call at Chatsworth House:
TM Travel 218 – Sheffield to Bakewell, via Chatsworth House; frequent daily service. **Hulleys 170** – Chesterfield to Bakewell; frequent daily service.
High Peak 58 – Macclesfield, Buxton, Monyash, Bakewell and Chatsworth House; twice daily in each direction on Sundays and Bank Holidays. Services 58, 170 and 218 also operate via Pilsley.

Facilities: As well as the amenities in Baslow: Chatsworth House provides shops, eating establishments and toilets in and around the stables.
Edensor Tea Cottage provides all you would expect from a traditional tea room.
Chatsworth Farm Shop, which also offers a café, is only a short distance from the walk. The Devonshire Arms at Pilsley.

Car Park: In addition to parking in Baslow, there is also a large car park at Chatsworth House; fees apply.

About the Walk

Entering Chatsworth Park via the former Eastmoor to Wardlow turnpike of 1759 and its bridge over Bar Brook, we pass the sites of two lost settlements – first Langley, and then, closer to the river crossing, Chatsworth. Passing Queen Mary's Bower, a 16th century construction once surrounded by a network of ponds, we arrive at the 1762 river crossing, affording magnificent views across the water to Chatsworth House and gardens.

We continue to Edensor, passing close by the remaining structures of the original village of the same name. The current settlement was constructed by Paxton and Robertson around 1830, giving the residents of Chatsworth House a sanitised view over the Derwent. Ascending an ancient packhorse way we head for Pilsley, changing direction at a guide stoop dated 1709. Descending towards Pilsley via a quiet lane, we cross the former 1812 Edensor to Ashford turnpike. The last ¼ of a mile to Pilsley is via an old grassy lane enclosed by walls.

Chatsworth House and park in the evening

From Pilsley we descend to Rymas Brook, crossing the former Chesterfield to Ashford turnpike, also of 1812. Then we climb again, crossing fields to reach the former Eastmoor to Wardlow turnpike of 1759 and then following its probable predecessor, a packhorse way, along which we descend to Bubnell. We cross the Derwent via a bridge dated 1603; the river crossing evidently predates the current ancient structure, since Dodd and Dodd quote an order from 1500 declaring that "no one shall henceforth lead or carry any millstones over the bridge at Basselowe under pain of 6s 8d to the lord for every pair of millstones so carried." Immediately beyond the bridge a watchman's shelter stands at an odd angle, opposite the "modern" replacement for the toll house that was demolished in 1872. The church of St Anne was originally constructed in the 13th to 15th centuries, but was restored by Paxton in 1852–3 and the chancel rebuilt by Stokes in 1911.

Queen Mary's Bower, Chatsworth Park

Directions

1. Starting from the Nether End area of Baslow, with your back to the toilet block, turn right along Church Lane and cross Bar Brook after around 80 yards.

2. Just beyond the bridge over Bar Brook, turn right along a metalled lane for 300 yards, passing Plantation Cottage as the lane veers to the left.

3. Passing through the turnstile to enter Chatsworth Park, continue along the crushed limestone track for a mile, passing White Lodge after 600 yards and Queen Mary's Bower just prior to Paine's Bridge.

4. Turn right to cross the Derwent, taking the path on your right immediately beyond the bridge. Continue along this well-made path for 650 yards, rising and falling to reach the roadside opposite the gateway to Edensor.

5. After crossing the busy B6012, negotiate the turnstile on the right of the cattle grid to enter the village of Edensor.

6. Follow the road to the right of the village green and St Peter's Church, continuing without deviation for a mile. The road becomes a track shortly after leaving the village. At the top of the lane, in the corner of the field on your right-hand side can be seen a guide stoop marking a junction of former packhorse routes, inscribed with Bakewell Road 1709, Chesterfield Rode and Sheffield Rode.

7. Turn right to follow Handley Lane for ¾ of a mile down to the B6048.

8. Cross the B6048 to the stile opposite, following the path across the field to a short flight of stone steps giving access to the walled lane beyond.

The Devonshire Arms, Pilsley

Baslow (upper inset map)

Bridge End
Site of Baslow Hydro
Bar Rd
Over End
20
Eaton Hill
School Ln
19
St Anne's Church
18
Watchman's shelter
A623
Baslow
START 1
Nether End
2
Cock Hill A619
A619
River Derwent
Baslow Village Hall
P

Main map

18
17
19
Baslow
St Anne's Church
START 1
2
Wheatlands Ln
A619
15
16
Peak and Northern Footpath Society sign No. 310
3
14
White Lodge
13
A619
B6012
Original course of Derwent
Lost village of Langley
12
Derwent Aqueduct (DVWB)
Pilsley
Devonshire Arms
10
11
Well
River Derwent
9
B6048
Chatsworth Farm Shop
8
Queen Mary's Bower
Stable Block
Paine's Bridge
4
P
Dunsa Ln
Chatsworth Institute
Chatsworth House
6
5
Edensor
7
St Peter's Church
Edensor Tea Cottage
Lost village of Edensor
Guide stoop
Approximate site of packhorse bridge and mill
B6012
Maud's Plantation
Barrow

9. Proceed along the grassy lane as it descends and curves to the right, reaching a picnic table after less than 300 yards. From here the lane has a metalled surface and rises a short distance to reach the village of Pilsley.

10. Descend High Street to the road junction, just beyond the Devonshire Arms.

11. Keep left to continue your descent for 300 yards. As you walk along the lane you will pass a well on your right-hand side.

12. Opposite a stone barn, take the footpath on your left, which crosses fields and descends steeply to the A619 Thirteen Bends road. Initially the path descends gradually, but after you negotiate the two closely-spaced pedestrian gates on your right the gradient increases. A further pedestrian gate leads to the crossing of a water course prior to the road.

13. Cross the busy A619 and take the footpath opposite, which immediately bridges Rymas Brook before you negotiate a stile leading to a steep ascent across pasture.

14. At the top of the ascent is a Peak and Northern Footpath Society sign No. 310 for Baslow, adjacent to a pedestrian gate. Follow the direction of the arrow for 340 yards to the corner of the field and a squeezer stile beside a gateway.

15. Turn right onto Wheatlands Lane, which was once the Eastmoor to Wardlow turnpike of 1759, an early route owned by the Chesterfield and Hernstone Lane Head Trust. Follow the lane for 60 yards.

Watchman's shelter, Baslow

16. Turn left at the pedestrian gate beside its larger sibling and cross the field, following a former wall line to reach a wall at right angles to your right.

17. Turn right and follow the path down to Bubnell, crossing several field boundaries as you go. This route was probably an earlier way between Bubnell and Hassop, superseded by the turnpike you walked along a few minutes ago. The path descends between buildings to emerge opposite Baslow Bridge.

18. Cross the Derwent via the bridge dated 1603/8/9 and turn right into Calver Road (A623).

19. At the mini roundabout, turn left up School Lane and follow it for almost 400 yards to the junction with Bar Road and Eaton Hill.

20. Turn right for the final 420 yards down Eaton Hill to the green.

Walk 7: Calton Lees – Beeley and Rowsley

Distance: 5½ miles   **Start:** The car park at Calton Lees

ESSENTIAL INFORMATION

Public Transport

Rowsley: Stagecoach 160 – four services in each direction from Matlock to Chatsworth, calling at Rowsley; Monday to Friday. **Trent Barton 6.1** – regular daily service between Derby and Bakewell. **Transpeak TP2 and TP3** – regular daily service between Derby and Buxton (change in Matlock).

Facilities: Chatsworth Garden Centre at Calton Lees offers a café and toilets within the retail establishment. Beeley offers the Devonshire Arms public house and the Old Smithy tea rooms. In Rowsley you'll find a pub, a hotel, shops within the Peak Village outlet shopping centre (with public toilet facilities), a post office and a village store.

Car Park: Calton Lees car park at Chatsworth Garden Centre; fees may apply. Rowsley: DDDC car park at Old Station Close (free).

About the Walk

Within a few hundred yards of the start of this walk we pass close by the remains of Chatsworth Estate's mill. Constructed for William Cavendish, the 4th Duke by James Paine in 1759, it replaced an older mill situated further

Beeley village

upstream and much closer to Chatsworth House, beside the former packhorse bridge. The mill continued in use until the 1950s, and then was badly damaged by a falling tree in 1962. Crossing One Arch Bridge, also built by Paine in 1759, we continue across parkland to reach the village of Beeley. The village is a popular attraction, boasting a tea room and pub. The church of St Anne was rebuilt in the early 1880s, although it retains traces dating back to the 12th century.

Beyond Beeley we take to the fields, following an ancient walled lane to Smeltingmill Wood beside the disued Burntwood Quarry. We pass between bridge abutments of the former quarry tramway before crossing Smeltingmill Brook via a substantial bridge. The large rocks on the opposite side of the valley are quarry spoil, no doubt dumped from the tramway above. Emerging on Rowsley Bar we ascend a short distance along the former Chesterfield to Rowsley Bridge turnpike of 1760; the toll bar cottage may be seen a short distance up the road.

Descending to Rowsley, we pass between the former terminus station of the Midland Railway and the site of a second station on the extension towards Bakewell and Manchester. Passing the former Railway Hotel we cross Rowsley Bridge, constructed in the 1400s and widened in the 1920s, which carried the former Wirksworth Moor to Longstone turnpike of 1759. Opposite the Peacock Hotel, a former manor house of the Haddon Estate bearing the date 1652, is an 1867 cast iron standard lamp, and set in the wall of Church Lane is a drinking fountain dated 1851 which is decorated during the annual well dressing celebrations. Returning over meadows to Calton Lees, we pass an architecturally interesting barn.

Directions

1. Starting with your back to Chatsworth Garden Centre, take the path out of the car park to the pedestrian and equestrian gates beside the cattle grid set into the surface of the B6012.

2. Cross the busy road and follow the path opposite, leading downhill towards the remains of Chatsworth's old flour mill.

3. Turn right, following the river downstream towards One Arch Bridge.

4. A few yards to the right of the bridge is a pedestrian gate, through which you must pass before turning left to cross the bridge. The traffic is light-controlled at the bridge crossing, so take your opportunity to cross the road.

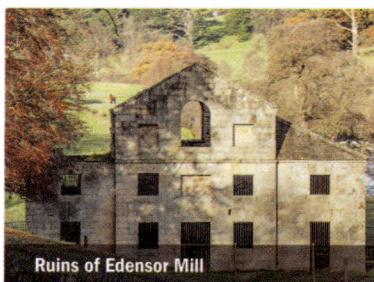
Ruins of Edensor Mill

5. Once over the bridge, negotiate the pedestrian gate on your right and follow the path across the large meadow to the B6012 around ½ a mile away, coming out opposite Church Lane in Beeley. As you crossed the meadow, you also crossed the Derwent Aqueduct.

6. Cross the busy B6012 and head up Church Lane, with St Anne's on your left and the former Vicarage on your right.

7. Turn right and keep right at the green and tree where the road forks, descending Chapel Hill towards the Devonshire Arms and Devonshire Square.

8. Facing the Devonshire Arms, turn left to follow Brookside and Beeley Brook upstream for 200 yards.

9. Where the lane forks, take the footpath over Beeley Brook and through the stile beyond. The path rises steeply at first, levelling out to cross a field and pass through a pedestrian gate which gives access to Chesterfield Road.

10. Cross Chesterfield Road to the pedestrian gate opposite. Once through the gate, follow the path, keeping the field boundary on your right, towards a cluster of farm buildings around 200 yards away.

11. Pass through the pedestrian gate on your right and immediately turn left to find a further pedestrian gate a few yards ahead of you, against a stone wall beside which you will walk. Along this short wooded section of path you will pass a pair of dwarf stoops, a squeezer stile that can be stepped over, before coming to a pedestrian gate that opens into a field.

12. Continue ahead, passing through two pedestrian gates set into hedges.

13. After around 40 yards, take the pedestrian gate on your left and immediately turn right. Continue in the same general direction as before for 200 yards, passing through a further two pedestrian gates set in stone walls.

14. Turn left up the walled track to Smeltingmill Wood around 260 yards away. Note the green Water Board gate on your right, which indicates the course of the Derwent Aqueduct.

15. On entering Smeltingmill Wood, follow the track for 70 yards as it climbs close to the left-hand boundary of the wood.

16. Take the path on your right, which continues to climb towards Fallinge. Close to the summit of the climb are two stone buttresses (see below), over which a tramway once ran from Burntwood Quarry on your left to tip unwanted stone down the valley side on your right.

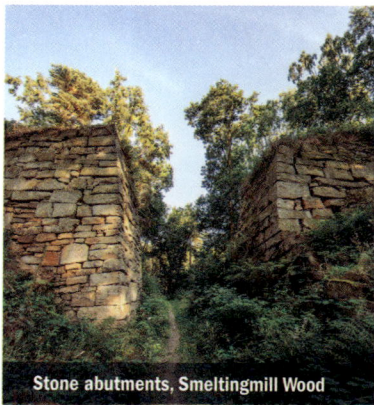

Stone abutments, Smeltingmill Wood

17. Take the right-hand fork which shortly crosses Smeltingmill Brook via a substantial wooden equestrian bridge. Follow the bridleway for around 300 yards.

18. Turn right onto the metalled track, which takes you to Rowsley Bar (Chesterfield Road).

19. Turn left up Rowsley Bar, noting the building ahead to your left which is the former toll house for the 1760 turnpike between Rowsley Bridge, Galdwin's Mark and Stanidge (Stone Edge). After only a few yards, before reaching the toll house, turn right and follow the path down to Little Rowsley.

20. Cross the B6012 Chatsworth Road at the busy junction with the A6. On your right is the original Midland Railway station. Follow the A6 towards Bakewell, passing the site of the second railway station on your left and the former railway hotel, now the Grouse and Claret, on your right. Cross the 15th century Rowsley Bridge over the River Derwent to Great Rowsley. Note the 1867 lamp standard on your left at the junction between the A6 and Woodhouse Road.

21. Immediately beyond the Peacock Hotel, turn right into Church Lane for 140 yards. Opposite the Peacock Hotel on Church Lane is a drinking fountain, erected in 1841 and decorated during the village well dressing festivities.

22. Opposite Home Farm take the track on your right, which soon passes beneath the former Midland Main Line. Follow the track to its end as it steadily meanders up- and downhill to the level of the Derwent.

23. As the walled track ends, continue into the field ahead for 200 yards, keeping the wall line on your left. Follow the path for a little over 100 yards through woodland, emerging into a large pasture.

A fine 18th century hay barn near Calton Lees

24. Walk across the field for 200 yards to the bank of the Derwent. Then strike out across the centre of the field in a similar direction, aiming for the gateway halfway between the Derwent on your right and Lindup Wood on your left.

25. Follow the grassy track across another large pasture for around ¼ of a mile.

26. After negotiating a stone stepped stile, climb steeply while getting closer to the field boundary on your left.

27. At the time of writing a dilapidated wooden ladder stile indicated the path's transition to the opposite side of the stone wall, currently facilitated by an open gateway. Follow the path around the perimeter of the field, keeping the field boundary within a few yards to your right.

28. At Calton Lees, cross the wall over a stone slab stile beside a gate. Descend the metalled lane for 150 yards, rising slightly to the crossroads.

29. Turn right, returning to Calton Lees car park after 400 yards, passing the garden centre on your right.

Walk 8: Calton Lees – Edensor

Distance: 4½ miles   **Start:** The car park at Calton Lees

ESSENTIAL INFORMATION

Public Transport

Calton Lees: Stagecoach 160 – Monday to Friday, 4 services in each direction from Matlock to Chatsworth.

Edensor: High Peak 58 – Sundays and Bank Holidays only, 2 services in each direction from Macclesfield, Buxton, Monyash and Bakewell.
Hulleys 170 – between Chesterfield and Bakewell; Monday to Friday, hourly service; Sundays and Bank Holidays, two-hourly service. **TM Travel 218** – hourly daily service, with exceptions, between Sheffield and Bakewell.

Facilities: Edensor Tea Cottage provides all you would expect from a traditional tea room.

Chatsworth Park

About the Walk

This short walk offers steep climbs, beautiful views and a little history. Leaving Calton Lees car park we follow a lane past Chatsworth Garden Centre and the hamlet of Calton Lees. Ascending to Calton Pastures via Calton Houses offers vistas along the Derwent Valley, and descending again to Edensor we pass Maud's Plantation and a round barrow, described in *The Burial Mounds of Derbyshire* as "75 foot in diameter and three foot in height." On our route through the manicured village of Edensor we pass the site of its former school and the only remaining building from the old village of the same name. Returning to Calton Lees via parkland on the west bank of the Derwent, we are treated to magnificent views of Chatsworth House across the water.

Directions

1. Facing the lane with your back to the car park, turn right.

2. Pass the garden centre on your left and continue along the metalled lane as it turns to the right. 150 yards beyond the tradesman's entrance to the garden centre you will reach a crossing of lanes, with the hamlet of Calton Lees behind you and to the left.

3. Continue ahead for around ¾ of a mile following the sign for Rye Croft and Pingle Cottage, noted on the OS map as Calton Houses. As you follow the lane, which runs alongside a stream, you will see a spring and stone trough on your right.

4. After negotiating the steep hairpins which lead to the cottages, take the lane that continues between and 100 yards beyond the dwellings to reach a gate leading back into the managed parkland.

5. Bear right and follow the path for just shy of 200 yards, keeping the wall line on your immediate right.

6. Once through the large pedestrian gate, follow the path to its intersection with a wide grassy track, with the Russian Cottage some 250 yards away to your right.

7. Continue ahead towards the gateway offering access to New Piece Wood.

8. Beyond the gate, follow the broad walled track that descends gently through the woodland.

9. Exit the wood via a similar gate to that by which you entered, and take a moment to enjoy the vistas up the Derwent Valley, of Chatsworth House and gardens, the Hunting Tower and the surrounding woods and parkland. Then descend through the deer park for 450 yards, with Maud's Plantation on your left.

Gardener's Cottage, the only surviving house from old Edensor village

10. With the spire of St Peter's church now visible, follow the path for 480 yards, heading slightly to the left of the steeple. 50 yards from the village, follow the direction arrow of the waymarker to head for the pedestrian gateway a few yards to the right of an electricity substation.

11. Negotiate the steps and gate, leading to another flight of steps descending to street level in the village of Edensor.

12. Turn right to follow the road for 240 yards down to the cattle grid at the entrance to the village.

13. Beyond the pedestrian turnstiles, cross the busy B6012.

14. Immediately opposite the road to Edensor is a wide crushed limestone path. Follow this for $\frac{1}{3}$ of a mile to Paine's Bridge.

15. Unless you are visiting Chatsworth House, do not cross the bridge. Instead, cross the road and follow the public footpath to a flight of steps cut into the hillside $\frac{1}{3}$ of a mile away. It is possible to follow the bank of the Derwent rather than the public right of way.

16. Climbing the steps, keep to the high ground and proceed ahead for almost $\frac{1}{2}$ a mile.

17. Re-cross the busy B6012 and turn left, descending the short distance to the pedestrian gateway giving access to the Carlton Lees car park.

18. Return the short distance to your starting location.

Haddon Hall

Haddon Hall, Pevsner's "English castle par excellence", stands on a limestone slope above the River Wye some 2 miles south of Bakewell. It was owned by the Vernon family since around 1170, passing to the Manners family by marriage in 1567, and was constructed almost entirely from materials from the landscape within which it stands – limestone and gritstone from the nearby moors, lead from local mines, and timber from the estate.

The exterior of Haddon Hall
(photo: courtesy of Haddon Hall)

The magnificent medieval banqueting hall, with its dais at one end, wooden screen at the other and minstrels' gallery above, was created around 1370 by Sir Richard de Vernon, a Crusader who fought in Gascony. One curiosity is a manacle attached to the screen; legend has it that if any guest "did not drink fayre" (i.e. drank either too much or too little) his wrist would be manacled and his drink poured down his sleeve. In the days before regular bathing when clothes might be worn for weeks on end, this would have been an effective deterrent to such undesirable behaviour!

The chapel may once have been the separate church of an early medieval village, Nether Haddon, lost to the Black Death in the 14th century. A chancel was added in 1427, and an octagonal spire in 1450; the fine medieval paintings adorning the walls were whitewashed during the Reformation, but were rediscovered in the early 20th century during the 9th Duke's restoration. The northwest tower, known as the Peveril or Eagle Tower, was added in 1530 by Sir George Vernon, called the King of the Peak because of his sumptuous lifestyle and lavish hospitality.

The Vernons were succeeded by the Manners family with the marriage of Dorothy Vernon, the second daughter of Sir George, to Sir John Manners, son of the 1st Earl of Rutland. The tale of Dorothy and John is a romantic one; it is told that they had a secret romance, but were forbidden to marry. They decided to elope, and one night around 1563, during one of her father's famous balls celebrating her sister's wedding, Dorothy escaped down a flight of steps, fleeing through the gardens and over a packhorse bridge to meet John, whereupon they rode away

The medieval chapel at Haddon Hall
(photo: courtesy of Haddon Hall)

and were married. Sadly there is little historical evidence to confirm these events, other than the fact that the couple did indeed marry, but the undeniably thrilling story captured the Victorian and Edwardian imaginations, and it became the subject of a series of novels, a play, a light opera by Sir Arthur Sullivan, and even a silent movie.

The excellent preservation of the house we see today is due, somewhat ironically, to the fact that it stood empty for 250 years, after the Manners family moved to their grander estate at Belvoir on their creation as Dukes of Rutland in 1703. Haddon's structure was maintained, but there was no significant modernisation until the 9th Duke embarked on a sensitive but thorough renovation programme in the early 20th century. This became his life's work, conducted to exacting standards and with a focus on restoring Haddon as closely as possible to its 17th century glory.

The Manners family had stakes in local quarries and lead mines, but when the railway came to Bakewell in the 1860s the 6th Duke of Rutland was concerned about the impact of this new form of transport on his carefully managed estate. He was influential in the construction of the Haddon Tunnel, a 1,058-yard (967-metre) underground stretch that opened in 1863 and carried the railway under and past the hall's immediate environs. (Compare with the 4th Duke of Devonshire, who moved the whole village of Edensor to avoid spoiling the idyllic pastoral view from Chatsworth!)

As well as restoring the fabric of the buildings, the 9th Duke set out to conserve many of the hall's furnishings. Notable among these were a fine collection of tapestries, which had remained hanging in the hall during its period of neglect. Fearing for their safety during the restoration work, the Duke moved them to the stable block, but in a disastrously ironic twist many of them were damaged or destroyed when a fire broke out there in 1925. Around 60 pieces were lost, but many others were restored and now hang in the house. The most important are a set of five tapestries representing 'The Five Senses'. These date from the early 17th century, were made by master weavers in Mortlake, and may well have belonged to Charles I; a set of 'Senses Tapestries' appears in the inventory of his possessions made after his execution in 1649.

One of the most charming parts of a visit to Haddon is its museum, consisting largely of everyday items discovered during the restoration of the hall. Exhibits like a child's shoe, coins, laundry tallies, cards and dice, all lost or discarded by generations past, are evocative of the many people who worked, visited or made their homes at Haddon – the ordinary folk as well as the lords and ladies.

The walks in the Haddon area will take you as far afield as Youlgrave, Stanton in Peak, Alport and the beautiful Lathkill Dale. As with the Chatsworth walks, neither include entry to the hall or gardens, but both pass close by, and you are encouraged to take the time for a visit if you can.

The Long Gallery inside Haddon Hall
(photo: courtesy of Haddon Hall)

Haddon Hall

Walk 9: Rowsley – Stanton in Peak and Haddon

Distance: 7 miles   **Start:** Old Station Close (car park), Rowsley

About the Walk

We start the walk from the site of the second Rowsley station, which opened on the new through line in 1862 and closed in 1967. Passing the former station hotel, now the Grouse and Claret, we cross Rowsley Bridge, constructed in the 1400s, widened in the 1920s and carrying the former Wirksworth Moor to Longstone turnpike of 1759. Turning left at the 1867 cast iron standard lamp, we head towards Caudwell's Mill, crossing the leat and the River Wye. Following the course of the Wye we make our way to Congreave, passing an ancient earthwork on the way. We ascend steeply to pass Stanton Old Hall on the way to Stanton village. On Pilhough Lane a convenient stone-flagged viewing platform offers a welcome seat and vistas up the Wye Valley, overlooking Haddon Hall.

Stanton in Peak is a pleasant village containing several listed structures, including the 1838 Holy Trinity church and the 18th century Flying Childers public house. We descend from the village into the valley of the River Lathkill via an ancient grassy lane lined with gnarled trees. After ascending the opposite side of the valley we enter a medieval field system in the vicinity of the lost village of Nether Haddon. Our descent into the Wye valley affords views of Haddon Hall nestled among the trees.

Skirting the Haddon Estate, we cross over Haddon Tunnel which once carried the former Midland Main Line, ensuring the residents of the Hall were not subject to the intrusive sight, sound and smell of passing trains; the construction of the tunnel was a condition of the railway's route across the Haddon Estate. We return to Rowsley via an old lane offering views along the valleys of the Wye, Lathkill and Derwent.

Directions

1. From the junction of Old Station Close and Dale Road North (the A6), head towards Bakewell past the northbound bus stop for the Transpeak and 6.1. The area now used as a car park was the site of the second railway station in Rowsley, while the Grouse and Claret was the station hotel. Continue over the 15th century Rowsley Bridge.

2. Turn left into Woodhouse Road, noting the listed Victorian lamp standard at the junction with Dale Road North. A few yards up Woodhouse Road you will pass the entrance to Caudwell's Mill; the current building dates from 1875 and replaced earlier buildings. Mills of various types have been documented on or around this site since the 1330s. Cross

Wye Bridge, which spans the mill race and the River Wye.

3. A few yards beyond the bridge, turn right along Peaktor Lane for around 300 yards, to the point where Peaktor Road swings dramatically to the left and starts to rise steeply. A few yards prior to the deviation in the road the remains of an old bridge may be seen on your right, with the outline of a cutwater clearly visible in the centre of the channel.

4. Proceed ahead through the pedestrian gate to the left of its big brother, following the grassy lane as it ascends and leaves the course of the river. Continue to follow this track until you meet a substantial earthen bank and ditch on your left. Follow the earthwork for 75 yards; the age and origin of this structure are unknown.

5. Locating the isolated footpath waymarker, leave the earthwork to your left and make your way across the field towards the bottom end of the woodland ahead.

6. After passing through the pedestrian gate, descend to a further gate and exit the woodland. A steep climb lies ahead for the short distance to a squeezer stile, located to the left of a gate. Follow the grassy track beyond, with the buildings of Dove House Farm on your right, to reach Congreave.

7. Turn left into Stantonhall Lane, ascending the steep climb beyond Stanton Old Hall, which you pass on your left. Continue your climb for a further 125 yards to reach a footpath on your right.

8. Climb up to the pedestrian gate and follow the path beyond as you continue your ascent towards Stanton. After 350 yards and a couple of pedestrian gates you will reach a flight of steps, which take you the final few feet up to Pilhough Lane.

9. Turn right towards Stanton and almost immediately pass a semi-circular walled and stone-flagged viewing platform to the right of the road. The platform contains a stone bench, offering the weary traveller a welcome resting place after the climb out of the Wye Valley and a chance to recover while admiring the view. Much of your route ahead can be seen from this vantage point. After your rest, follow the lane for ⅓ of a mile to Stanton in Peak.

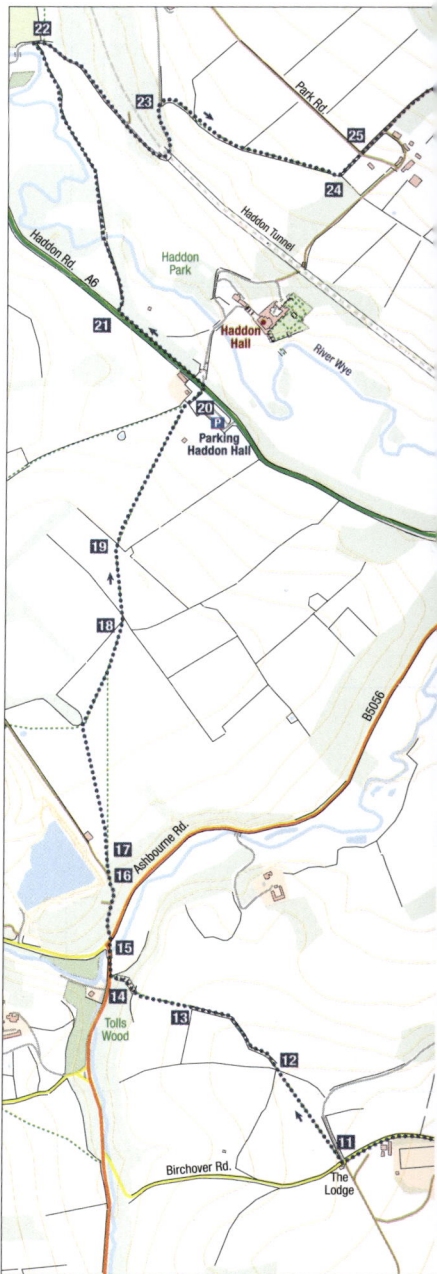

27

26

Church Ln

St Katherine's Church

River Derwent

Peak Village

Grouse and Claret

START

1

Peacock Hotel

A6 Rowsley

28

2

Site of 2nd Rowsley Stn

River Wye

3

Stantonhall Ln

4

5

Peaktor Ln

Dove House Farm

7

6

Congreave

8

Pilhough

9

Pilhough Rd

Beighton Houses

Pilhough Ln

Flying Childers Inn

Holy Trinity Church

10

Stanton in Peak

Stanton Hall

A bird's-eye view of Stanton in Peak

10. Turn right down Main Road, passing Holy Trinity church on your left, shortly followed by the Flying Childers public house also on your left. Middle Street continues in front of the Flying Childers, but you should keep right down the main road, now Birchover Road, for a further ¼ of a mile. A high stone wall encloses the left side of the road as you exit the village, until you reach North Lodge on the Stanton Estate and a crossing of lanes.

11. Take the footpath on your right across the field, signposted for Hawleys Bridge.

12. Follow the rough tree-lined grassy track downhill for around 250 yards, until the track makes a 90° turn to the right.

13. Continue ahead through the field to Tolls Wood. Once through the pedestrian gate, descend the steps beside the quarry on your left. You emerge from the wood beside the B5056.

14. Turn right for a short distance up the roadside and over Hawley Bridge (dated 1775) crossing the River Lathkill.

15. Cross Ashbourne Road and follow the metalled lane opposite, which rises steeply. Around 120 yards up the hill is a gateway across the lane, shortly beyond which is a footpath and wooden guide post on your right.

16. Take this path which rises above the lane, to a pedestrian gateway leading into a field.

17. Head for the promontory of trees and area of rough ground 300 or so yards ahead. On reaching the trees, turn right and head for the top corner of the field.

18. Pass through a squeezer stile and after a few yards a pedestrian gate, following the path for 170 yards to a rather snug squeezer stile.

19. Descend through the pasture, making sure to admire the magnificent views over the Wye Valley to Haddon Hall, heading for the bottom left corner of the field. Take the track through the gate to Haddon Road (the A6).

20. Cross the A6 and turn left, following the pavement for 200 yards to where a gap in the hedge and stile in the stone wall to your right mark the entrance to a footpath.

21. Follow the footpath for around ½ a mile, during which it descends to and crosses the Wye before emerging on a metalled lane.

22. Turn right and follow the lane as it rises alongside the former Midland Main Line. After 400 yards the mouth of Haddon Tunnel may be seen on your left, immediately prior to the lane swinging to the left to pass over the tunnel. Continue for a further 120 yards, to the point where a number of notices indicate that the lane ahead is private.

23. Climb up the embankment on your right, passing through the equestrian gate and following the path for ¼ of a mile along the field boundary to your right. Beyond the second gate you enter a grassy track.

24. There is no alternative but to turn left, following the track as it rises to meet the metalled Park Road.

25. Follow Park road for ⅓ of a mile, as far as a T junction.

The Peacock, Rowsley

26. Turn left, following the lane for 250 yards to where the ways part. Views down the valley to your left are towards Coombs Farm, Coombs Viaduct and Bakewell.

27. Take the lare to your right and follow it for 1¼ miles, ascending to woodland, before making the long descent back to Rowsley, offering views over the Wye Valley and down the Derwent Valley; you should be able to trace the first half of the walk across the landscape. Upon reaching Rowsley village the track becomes Church Lane, with the church of St Katherine on your left. Shortly afterwards you pass the abutments of what must have been a rather low bridge carrying the former Midland Main Line.

28. At the end of Church Lane, with the Peacock Hotel on your left and a drinking fountain dated 1841 on your right, turn left and retrace your steps to your starting point beyond the river bridge.

Walk 10: Youlgrave, Haddon and Alport

Distance: 5½ miles   **Start:** All Saints Church, Youlgrave

ESSENTIAL INFORMATION

Public Transport: Hulleys 172 – Mondays to Saturdays, Bakewell to Matlock via Youlgrave.

Facilities: The village of Youlgrave offers public toilets, three pubs, a post office and general stores, a bakery, and accommodation ranging from hostel to hotel.

Car Park: Off-street parking (with public toilet facilities) is at Coldwell End, around ½ a mile from the start of the walk.

About the Walk

Leaving the environs of All Saints Church in Youlgrave (often alternatively spelled Youlgreave – the two are used interchangeably locally) we follow the route of an ancient trackway to Coalpit Packhorse Bridge. Rising to Haddon Fields, we emerge from the tree line close to Bowl Barrow,

Church Street, Youlgrave

opened by the antiquary William Bateman in 1824 and documented in 1848 by his son Thomas in *Vestiges of the Antiquities of Derbyshire*.

For the next mile or so we pass through the remains of a medieval field system, crossing the conjectural path of the Portway and a Roman road connecting Derby and the High Peak. The route offers magnificent views over the Wye Valley, Haddon Hall and, a little further along, Lathkill Dale, as we proceed towards Stanton in the Peak and its Hall.

Skirting the disused Shiningbank Quarry, we descend to the attractive hamlet of Alport, with numerous bridges and a mill, before returning to Youlgrave beside the River Bradford, our path overshadowed by impressive limestone cliffs and passing a former packhorse bridge and a lead mine adit across the water. Beyond the slab bridge at Bradford we ascend the valley side to Youlgrave Hall, with the route back to our starting location taking us past numerous interesting listed structures including the village cistern, constructed at the behest of the Youlgrave Friendly Society of Women in 1829.

Directions

1. From the crossroads beside All Saints Church, take Conksbury Lane for around 250 yards, passing the George Hotel on your right.

2. Just prior to Easter Cottage, turn right and follow Coalpit Lane for a little over ⅓ of a mile to the River Lathkill, passing Raper Lodge on your right.

3. Cross the River Lathkill via Coalpit Bridge and begin your ascent through Lathkill Bank Plantation. As the slope gets steeper please ignore the OS map or similar and follow the accompanying map; the route ahead has been diverted for years, and a sign in the undergrowth will also direct you appropriately. The path doglegs to the left, providing a more gentle way through the wood.

4. After negotiating the equestrian gate, take the path in the 2 o'clock direction, heading for the copse on the brow of the hill.

5. Once through the equestrian gate, follow the path ahead, but notice the rather ornate cast iron supports for the barn roof here. Continue across Haddon Fields for a little over a mile, the path becoming a track as it nears Haddon.

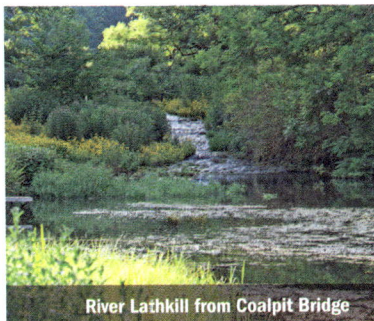

River Lathkill from Coalpit Bridge

Sweeping vistas over the Wye Valley and Haddon Hall open up along this section of the walk.

6. Prior to the gate permitting access to Haddon Hall's car park and the A6, turn back on yourself, aiming towards the top-left corner of the field, currently out of sight over the brow of the hill. The official path takes you roughly over the bumps in the landscape, to the right of the stone barn. However, if you follow the track a footpath sign will direct you up the wall line to your intended waypoint. When you get to the top, look back to take advantage of the views up the valley.

7. Once the squeezer stile has been negotiated, turn left across the field for 170 yards to a pedestrian gateway, and follow the direction arrow to the left to another squeezer stile shortly afterwards.

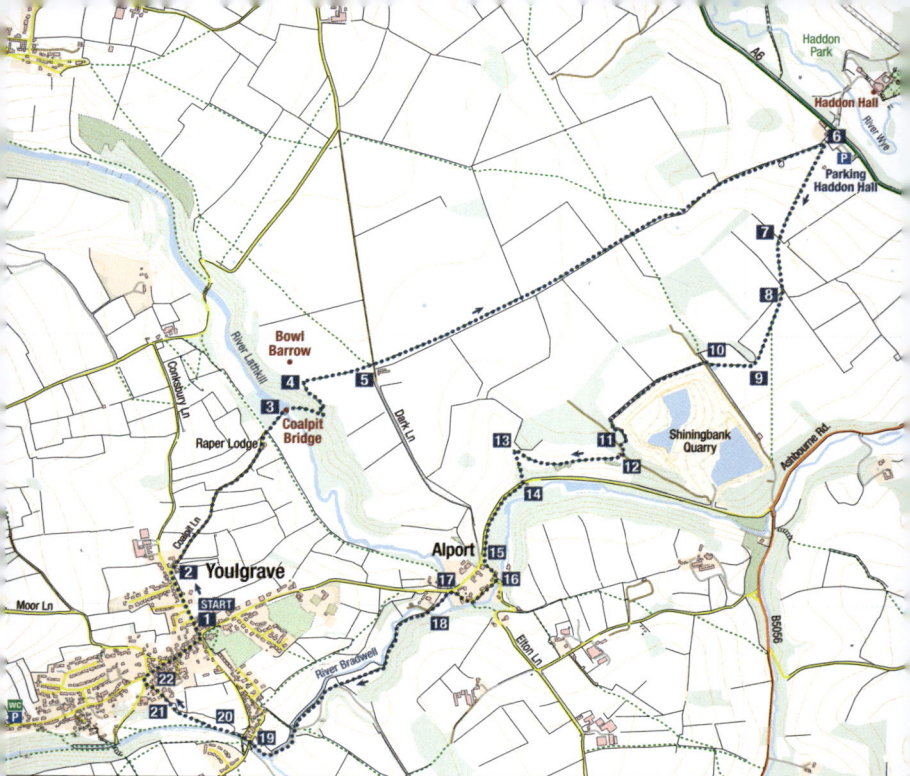

8. With your back to the stile, strike out across the field in a 2 o'clock direction, heading for the left edge of the line of mature trees jutting out into the field. Among the trees are a couple of shafts from a long-abandoned lead mine.

9. At the tree line, head for the dew pond in a 1 o'clock direction from the line of trees.

10. Cross the lane and take the footpath opposite, skirting Shiningbank Quarry on your left for around ¼ of a mile and descending to a track.

11. Turn left onto the track for a short distance. A prominent sign alerts you to the dangers of quarry workings and also indicates a footpath to your right.

12. Descend the short but steep footpath to a wooden stile and open fields, with views over the River Lathkill. Again, ignore the OS map for the next few hundred yards, in order to avoid a steep drop. Instead, follow the path, which becomes a grassy track, to a yellow-topped marker post.

13. Turn left down the dale to reach Alport Lane (the B5056).

14. Cross the road to the pavement opposite and turn right towards Alport for around 350 yards.

Alport village

15. Turn left down Dark Lane, with the former mill on your left.

16. Prior to the stone bridge over the Lathkill, turn right onto Elton Lane which shortly returns you to the B5056.

17. Keep left, crossing the 1793 bridge over the Lathkill, and then immediately take the footpath on your left which descends to the level of the River Bradford via a metalled lane.

18. Cross the Bradford and follow the limestone path to Mawstone Lane, around ½ a mile and a further river crossing upstream.

19. Cross Mawstone Lane and take the limestone path opposite. Continue for 150 yards.

20. Take the right-hand path, which rises steeply up the side of Bradford Dale.

21. The path becomes a lane, known as Brookleton, which you follow the short distance to its junction with Holywell Lane. Public toilets are a short distance down the hill on your left. Otherwise, turn right for a short distance up to Main Street.

22. Turn right along Main Street, passing the cistern on your left and the youth hostel, pub and post office on your right, returning to All Saints Church a few yards beyond.

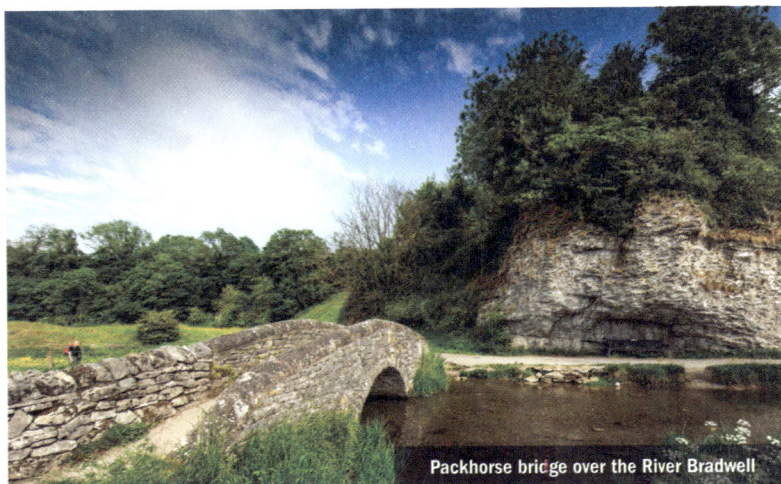
Packhorse bridge over the River Bradwell

Bibliography

Curlew's Peak District Collection

Curlew Press offers a growing collection of guides and walking books to the Peak District, available direct from the publisher and from selected bookshops and giftshops in the area. These include:

Souvenir and Walker's Guide to Buxton and the Goyt Valley by Louise Maskill (2021)

Souvenir and Walker's Guide to Cromford by Louise Maskill (2020)

Souvenir and Walker's Guide to the Derwent Valley: Matlock to Derby by Karl Barton (2022)

Souvenir and Walker's Guide to Hartington by various (2023)

Souvenir and Walker's Guide to the Hope Valley by Louise Maskill (2021)

The Spa Waters of Derbyshire by Louise Maskill (2021)

Walks Around the High Peak Trail by Karl Barton (2020, revised and updated 2023)

Walks Around the Tissington Trail by Karl Barton and Mark Titterton (2020, reprinted 2023)

Other sources

Black's Guide to Derbyshire (Adam and Charles Black, 1895)

Derbyshire Historic Environment Record, available at her.derbyshire.gov.uk

Derbyshire Place Names by Anthony Poulton-Smith (Sutton, 2005)

Haddon Hall by Bryan Cleary (Heritage House Group, 2005)

Haddon Hall by Keith H. Mantell (English Life Publications, 1987)

Historic England, available at www.historicengland.org.uk

Industrial Archaeology of the Peak District by Helen Harris (Ashbourne Editions, 1971)

Peak Place-Names by Louis McMeeken (Halsgrove, 2003)

Peakland Roads and Trackways by A.E. Dodd and E.M. Dodd (Moorland Publishing Company, 1974)

The Buildings of England: Derbyshire by Nikolaus Pevsner (Penguin Books, 1953)

The Derbyshire Country House by Maxwell Craven and Michael Stanley (Breedon Books, 1991)

The Industrial Archaeology of Derbyshire by Frank Nixon (David & Charles, 1969)

The Peak of Derbyshire by John Leyland (Seeley & Co., 1891)

The Place-names of Derbyshire, Part 1: High Peak Hundred by Kenneth Cameron (CUP, 1959)

Your Guide to Chatsworth by Sally Ambrose, Matthew Hirst and Steve Porter (Chatsworth House Trust, 2015)